Contents

September 11 2001 5

Terrorism on US soil 9

History of the World Trade Center 17

Islam and the USA 20

Behind the attacks 25

Stories from ground zero 29

Looking ahead: war on terrorism 36

Countries that lost citizens in the WTC attack 44

Glossary 46

Resources 47

Index 48

September 11 2001

TERRORISTS ATTACK THE U.S.A

www.raintreepublishers.co.uk

Visit our website to find out more information about **Raintree** books.

To order:

 Phone 44 (0) 1865 888112

 Send a fax to 44 (0) 1865 314091

 Visit the Raintree Bookshop at www.raintreepublishers.co.uk to browse our catalogue and order online.

First published in Great Britain by Raintree, Halley Court, Jordan Hill, Oxford OX2 8EJ, part of Harcourt Education. Raintree is a registered trademark of Harcourt Education Ltd.

Editorial: Nick Hunter, Catherine Clarke and Jo Waters
Design: Joanna Sapwell (www.tipani.co.uk)
Production: Lorraine Hicks

Originated by Dot Gradations Ltd
Printed and bound in Hong Kong, China by South China Printing Company Limited

ISBN 1 844 21088 X (hardback)
06 05 04 03 02
10 9 8 7 6 5 4 3 2 1

ISBN 1 844 21089 8 (paperback)
07 06 05 04 03
10 9 8 7 6 5 4 3 2 1

British Library Cataloguing in Publication Data

Lalley, Patrick
September 11 2001: terrorists attack the US.
973.9'31
A full catalogue record for this book is available from the British Library.

Acknowledgements
The publishers would like to thank the following for permission to reproduce photographs: Abdul Majeed Goraya p. **38**; AFP Photo Files p. **28**; Banaras Khan p. **24**; Beth Kaiser p. **36**; Corbis (Robert Schmidt) p. **6**; Craig Ellerbroek pp. **16**, **19**; Dan Joyce p. **8**; David and Peter Turnley p. **23**; Eric Feferberg pp. **35**, **39**; FBI Photo p. **12**; Jeff Mitchell p. **43**; Lee Celano p. **31**; Mohammad Bashir p. **40**; New York Daily News (Mike Albans) p. **32**; Reuters New Media Inc. p. **26**; Sean Adair p. **11**; Stephen Jaffe p. **7**; Tim Shaffer p. **14**; Towers Kelly (Mooney Photography) p. **4**; United States Navy p. **27**.

Cover photograph reproduced with permission of Corbis (Roberto Schmidt).

Content consultants: Sean Dolan and Leigh Ann Cobb.

Every effort has been made to contact copyright holders of any material reproduced in this book. Any omissions will be rectified in subsequent printings if notice is given to the publishers.

September 11 2001

Tuesday September 11, 2001, began as a beautiful morning in New York City. It was a normal late-summer day in the largest city in the USA. The temperature was warm, and the sky was bright and clear as New Yorkers began their morning rush hour – the time between 7:00 and 9:00 a.m. when millions of them make their way from home to work.

But by a few minutes after 9:00 a.m., the sky had turned dark with smoke, dust and debris. Two passenger airliners, **hijacked** by religious **extremists**, smashed into the twin towers of the World Trade Center (WTC) and exploded.

The first crash happened a few minutes before 9:00 a.m., the second 18 minutes later. By 10:30 a.m., both of the 110-storey buildings had collapsed.

About the same time, two other aeroplanes were also hijacked. One was crashed deliberately into the Pentagon in Washington, D.C. The Pentagon is the headquarters of the US Defense Department, the agency of government that controls the military.

The fourth aeroplane crashed into an open field in western Pennsylvania. Some people on that aeroplane called family members and friends on mobile telephones and told them what was

◄ **The World Trade Center's twin towers, seen here behind the Statue of Liberty, dominated the world-famous New York skyline.**

▲ Members of the New York Police Department work at ground zero, as the site of the ruins of the World Trade Center came to be known.

happening. It is believed the hijackers intended to crash the fourth aeroplane into a target in Washington, D.C. Passengers aboard the aeroplane apparently struggled with the hijackers and forced the plane to crash on to open grassland, so no one else would be injured.

That night, President George W. Bush told the American people he would bring to justice whoever planned the hijackings. Less than one month later, the USA began bombing the country of Afghanistan. The USA said that Afghanistan's government was providing shelter to a rich Saudi Arabian named Osama bin Laden, whom it was believed headed the terrorist organization responsible for the hijackings.

Together, the World Trade Center and the Pentagon symbolized US economic and military power in the world. The attack on the twin towers and the Pentagon, resulted in almost 3000 deaths. The USA saw the attack as an act of war. Within days, President Bush announced the US intention to fight its own war against **terrorism** worldwide.

The war would probably be a long one, Bush told the American people in a televised speech to a joint session of **Congress** on 20 September. 'Americans should not expect one battle,' the president said, 'but a lengthy campaign unlike any other we have ever seen.' Bush vowed to Americans that 'we will direct every resource at our command … to the disruption and defeat of the global terror network.'

▲ **Firefighters assess the damage at the site of the terrorist attack on the Pentagon on September 11, 2001. This section of the Pentagon had recently been renovated and housed US Army offices.**

Terrorism on US soil

American Airlines flight 11 left Boston, Massachusetts, for Los Angeles, California, on the morning of September 11, 2001. The plane was a Boeing 767 with 92 people on board. Shortly after take-off, five men, armed with box-cutters, took control of the plane. They set its course for New York City, where at 8:45 a.m. it was deliberately crashed into the north tower of the World Trade Center. The impact ripped a huge hole in the side of the building. The thousands of gallons of jet fuel on board acted as a bomb, setting off a huge explosion and fire.

At this point, many of the thousands of people who worked in the buildings started to evacuate. Firefighters, police and emergency medical personnel rushed to the scene to control the fire, help the injured, and clear the buildings. At that point, most people thought it had been a terrible accident, not a terrorist attack.

At about the same time as flight 11's **hijacking**, five hijackers took over United Airlines flight 175, also a 767 bound for Los Angeles from Boston. This flight had 65 people on board.

At 9:03 a.m., flight 175 hit the south tower and exploded. President Bush was visiting a school in Florida at the time. After being informed of the incidents, he said the USA had suffered 'an apparent terrorist attack.'

◀ **United Airlines flight 175 seen as it is about to hit the south tower of the World Trade Center on Tuesday September 11, 2001.**

After the second crash, the US government ordered all aeroplanes in US airspace to land. No aeroplanes were allowed to take-off for two days afterwards, until the government felt sure no more terrorist attacks were likely. It was the first time in US history that such action had been taken. People across the country were stranded at airports.

Afraid that the country would come under further attack, the government immediately put the military on the highest level of alert. The president was flown to Air Force bases in Louisiana and Nebraska for safety. Air Force fighter jets patrolled the skies over New York and two aircraft carriers sailed to New York harbour. The Capitol building in Washington, D.C. was evacuated.

'Make no mistake,' President Bush said while in Louisiana, 'the United States will hunt down and punish those responsible for these cowardly acts.'

The towers collapse

Two passenger jets colliding with the twin towers was a huge disaster in itself. The crash, and the explosions and fires that followed killed many people instantly. People who worked in the towers above the site of the crashes were trapped. (The planes crashed into the 94th to 99th floors of the north tower and into the 78th to 84th floors of the south tower.) Many of those trapped, jumped to their deaths from the buildings.

Meanwhile, the thousands of people who worked on the floors below the crash were trying to get out. Hundreds of firemen and policemen were rushing into the buildings to rescue those inside. People who got out said they saw firefighters racing up the stairs to help while everyone else was hurrying down to escape.

Then things got worse.

▲ The south tower of the World Trade Center burst into flames after being struck by a hijacked plane. The north tower burned from the earlier attack.

At 10:05 a.m., the south tower collapsed. Each plane was carrying more than 10,000 gallons of jet fuel. That fuel exploded in the crash, setting off fires that may have burned as hot as 1090°C. The fire was so hot that it weakened the building's structure. The weight of the floors above the fire pushed down on the weak spots. Those floors collapsed onto the floors below them, which in turn caved in the lower floors. The building collapsed in on itself in what engineers call 'a pancake effect.' Once the process began, it took only 15 seconds for the building to come down.

Thousands of people were able to get out before the building fell; but there were thousands still inside who died. The collapse created a huge cloud of dust, smoke and debris that covered the

▲ An aerial photograph shows the damage caused by the crash of hijacked Flight 77 into the Pentagon.

streets of lower Manhattan near the World Trade Center. The grey dust blocked out the Sun and covered everything in its path.

People were still trying to get away when the north tower collapsed at 10:28 a.m. A second menacing cloud covered the streets and buildings.

Eventually, fire and structural damage destroyed all seven buildings in the World Trade Center complex. Nearly 3000 people died in the New York attacks, including more than 400 police and firefighters, who were killed as they rushed to help.

Pentagon attacked

The attack on the World Trade Center was shocking in itself; but the terrorists were not finished.

At 9:43 a.m. American Airlines flight 77 crashed into the Pentagon, which is just across the Potomac River from Washington, D.C. The Boeing 757 had left Dulles Airport in Washington and was bound for Los Angeles with 64 people on board. Once again, five men took control of the aeroplane. They then deliberately crashed it into the Pentagon.

On a typical day more than 24,000 people work in the Pentagon. Besides the passengers on the aeroplane, 125 people on the ground were killed. The building was evacuated after the crash. At about 10:10 a.m. part of the building collapsed.

The Pentagon is not only one of the largest office buildings in the world, it is also one of the most unusual. Most buildings are four-sided. The Pentagon has five sides, surrounding five interior wings. The hallways go all the way around the building and are connected to each other by ten corridors that intersect the wings like spokes on a wheel.

The damage at the Pentagon could have been much worse. The part of the building where the aeroplane hit had recently been rebuilt to make it stronger. During reconstruction, special blast-resistant windows, fire sprinklers and steel columns had been added. Those improvements helped to save hundreds of lives. When the aeroplane hit, the building did not collapse straight away and the fire did not spread. If the terrorists had hoped to make more than a symbolic attack on the nerve centre of the US military, then the attack on the Pentagon was a failure. There was a great loss of life and tremendous economic damage, but at no point was the command structure of the US armed forces affected.

Crash in Pennsylvania

The terrorists did not succeed in carrying out all their plans. United Airlines flight 93 was bound from Newark, New Jersey, to San Francisco, California. But after hijackers took over the flight, the Boeing 757 set a course towards Washington, D.C.

Investigators think the hijackers wanted to crash the aeroplane into a symbol of the government, such as the White House, the Capitol or Camp David.

Some of the people on the plane used mobile telephones to call friends or relatives. The passengers said four men took over the aeroplane. The people on the ground told them that three other aeroplanes had been hijacked and crashed. Several passengers said that they knew they were going to die but that they were going to try to stop the hijacking. 'I'm on a plane, it's United flight 93, and we've been hijacked,' Thomas E. Burnett, Jr., told his wife over the phone. 'They've knifed a guy, and there's a bomb on board.' Though the hijackers claimed to have a bomb, it is now believed they were armed only with box-cutters. 'We're going to do something,' Burnett told his wife. 'I've got to go ... if they are going to run this plane into the ground, we're going to do something.'

Nobody knows for sure what happened after that. Investigators believe the passengers fought with the hijackers, making the aeroplane crash into an open field in western Pennsylvania. Everyone on board was killed, but many more lives would have been lost if the hijackers had succeeded in crashing the airliner into an occupied building in a crowded city.

◄ **Smoke rises behind investigators as they comb the crater left by the crash of United Airlines flight 93 near Shanksville, Pennsylvania.**

History of the World Trade Center

When they were completed, the twin towers of the World Trade Center were the world's tallest buildings. Construction on the towers began in 1966. The first tenants moved into offices in December 1970, but the ribbon-cutting ceremony to mark the official opening of the new buildings was not held until 4 April 1973.

The architect was Minoru Yamasaki. The owners wanted over 1 million square metres of office space. Yamasaki did not see a practical way to design a building with that much space. He did not like the idea of many smaller buildings, so he decided to design two towers, each 110 stories (just over 410 metres) tall.

A building that tall must be specially designed. The World Trade Center complex would be built on 16 acres at the tip of Manhattan, which is an island at the mouth of the Hudson River in New York Bay. This meant the building would have to be able to withstand the high winds and storms that sometimes blow into New York City off the Atlantic Ocean.

The design Yamasaki picked was very simple. The towers were

◄ **The World Trade Center towers were symbols of US power and financial strength.**

perfectly square. Each wall was 63 metres wide. The outside of the towers was covered by a frame of 36-centimetre-wide steel columns. The centre of the steel columns were 1 metre apart. These exterior walls supported the main weight of the building. The interior centre of the building was a hollow steel core, in which lifts and stairwells were placed. This kind of skyscraper design is called a tube building.

The lifts were a particular challenge. The World Trade Center had a unique system that saved space. Special 'express' lifts took passengers to 'sky lobbies' on the 41st and 74th floors. From there different lifts took people to floors between the sky lobbies, the roof and the ground.

Yamasaki wanted people to be able to look at the towers from the ground. If people are too close to a tall structure like the Empire State Building, they cannot see it very well. This meant there needed to be an open area around the base of the World Trade Center. So Yamasaki designed an open plaza, protected from the wind on each side by five-storey buildings.

New York city skyline

The twin towers quickly became recognized as a symbol of New York City. The towers were at the tip of Manhattan, close to the Statue of Liberty. Millions of people went to the viewing platform on top of one of the towers to see the city and the ocean. On a clear day, you could see over 70 kilometres in each direction.

The skyline of New York City is famous around the world. The towers appeared on postcards, in films and on television. In a remake of the classic monster film *King Kong*, the giant ape scaled one of the towers. (In the original film, King Kong climbed the Empire State Building.) On 7 August 1974, a French daredevil named Phillippe Petit walked a tightrope cable strung between the two towers. Three years later, George Willig, a rock climber who called

▲ The twin towers were perhaps the most recognizable landmark on the Manhattan skyline.

himself the 'human fly', instantly became famous by climbing the outside of one of the towers.

As its name suggests, the World Trade Center was a headquarters for international business. People from more than 80 countries worked there (see pages 44–45). Hundreds of companies rented space in the towers. Among these were many of the investment banks and brokerage houses that served on nearby Wall Street, the home of the US stock market.

'The World Trade Center should, because of its importance, become a representation of man's belief in humanity, his need for individual dignity, his beliefs in cooperation of men, and through cooperation, his ability to find greatness,' Yamasaki said.

Islam and the USA

The 19 men who hijacked the aeroplanes were Muslims, which means they follow a religion called Islam. Islam began on the Arabian Peninsula in the 7th century. The people who organized and carried out the attack argue that their acts were justified by their religious beliefs, but most Muslims would not agree.

Like Christianity and Judaism, Islam holds that there is only one god. Muslims call this god Allah.

Muslims believe that Allah's truths were revealed directly to a man named Muhammad (pbuh) by the angel Jibril. These truths were recorded in the 114 chapters of Islam's holy book, the Koran. Muhammad (pbuh), who lived on the Arabian Peninsula between AD 570 and 632, is the **prophet** and founder of Islam. Muslims also recognize some of the important figures of Christianity and Judaism, such as Abraham, Moses and even Jesus Christ, as prophets.

Islam is one of the fastest-growing religions in the world. It is estimated there are 1.2 billion Muslims in the world, including 7 million Muslims in the USA. About 20 per cent of the world's Muslims live in Arabic-speaking nations. Indonesia, an island country in southeast Asia, is the country that is home to the most Muslims. Around the world Islam, like any other major religion, includes many different beliefs and groups within it.

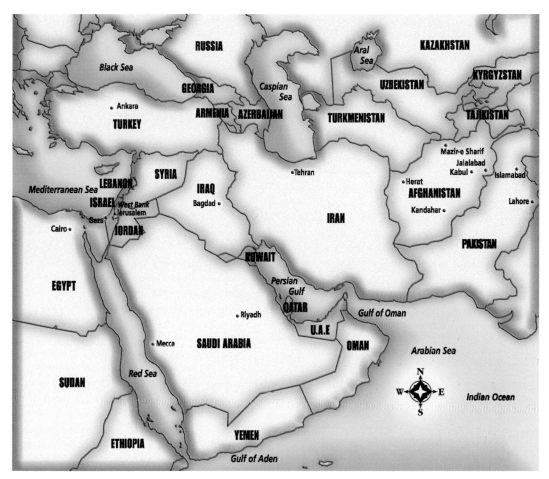

▲ The Middle East is important for many reasons, but primarily for its huge deposits of oil.

Islamic extremism

Investigators believe the hijackers belonged to an Islamic terrorist organization called al-Qaeda, which is Arabic for 'the base'. Al-Qaeda was headed by Osama bin Laden, and it was allied with many other terrorist organizations throughout the Islamic world.

Bin Laden and his followers believe in a very radical, or extreme, version of Islam. Many Muslims do not agree with al-Qaeda's views. Bin Laden believes that the Koran allows, or even requires, Muslims to attack non-muslim targets, even if innocent people are killed.

They argue that the USA in particular is an enemy of Islam because they stationed troops in Saudi Arabia, which, as the home of Muhammad (pbuh), Muslims regard as a sacred land. They believe it should be preserved only for the followers of Islam.

One of the most important influences on Islamic **extremists** like those of al-Qaeda is the work of a man named Muhammad ibn al-Wahhab. Al-Wahhab lived from 1703 to 1792 in what is now Saudi Arabia. He believed that Islam needed to be 'purified' of the ideas and practices added to it after the death of the prophet Muhammad (pbuh). Al-Wahhab condemned any version of Islam that developed after that time. His followers, usually referred to as Wahhabis by non-Muslims, are still among the most influential leaders in the Middle East. The royal family of Saudi Arabia, for example, consider themselves to be Wahhabis.

Another influence on bin Laden is Sayyid Qutb, an Egyptian Muslim. In his writings, Qutb argued that Islam had to be a complete way of life, governing all aspects of human society and individual behaviour. The greatest threats to Islam, he believed, were modern societies such as the USA and the Soviet Union because their laws and governments were not based on religion. Qutb was executed by the Egyptian government in 1966.

At the time of the World Trade Center attacks the government of Afghanistan was called the Taliban. Taliban is a word which means 'religious student'; and was used to refer to the government in Afghanistan because many of its leaders had been trained in special religious Islamic schools, called madrashahs, in Pakistan. During the 1980s these people resisted the Soviet Union's occupation of Afghanistan and afterwards had tried to make all of Afghan society conform to their view of Islam.

The Middle East

Although the majority of the world's Muslims are not Arab, much of the turmoil arising from Islamic extremism has been centred in the Middle East. The Middle East is a term used for the countries of north-east Africa and south-west Asia. Almost all of the Middle East is Arab or Muslim or both.

Much of the conflict in the Middle East is between Arab countries and Israel. Israel was founded in 1948 as a homeland for the world's Jews on land which was previously known as Palestine. This territory was also claimed by local Arabs of the region, who are still known as

▲ **This Muslim man is preparing to bow in the direction of the holy city of Mecca as he prays.**

Palestinians. In the following decades these rival claims have caused several wars between Israel and its Arab neighbours, all of which Israel has won. As a result, Israel has occupied more Arab land. This has led to an even greater displacement of the Palestinian population. An estimated 2 million Palestinians live as **refugees** throughout this disputed region.

In their struggle for a homeland and against Israel, the Palestinians have often used **terrorism**. In recent years, this has often taken the form of 'suicide bombings' by young Palestinians. Many of them share an extremist interpretation of Islam with other Islamic **fundamentalist** groups including al-Qaeda. Its suicide bombers set off explosives on their bodies in crowded public places, killing themselves and many Israelis in the process. They believe that such actions are justified as what the Koran calls jihad (struggle) against infidels (those who do not believe in Islam) who oppress Muslims. In this case, they regard the oppressors as Israel and its rich and powerful chief supporter, the USA. The bombers regard themselves as **martyrs** for Islam who will be instantly rewarded upon their death with a place next to Allah in Paradise. The hijackers in the World Trade Center and Pentagon attacks held similar views.

Behind the attacks

Al-Qaeda's attack on the World Trade Center and the Pentagon was inspired by the idea of jihad. But September 11 2001, or 9.11.01 as it is known in the USA, was not the first time that Islamic terrorists had attacked the World Trade Center. On 26 February 1993 a truck bomb exploded in a parking garage beneath the World Trade Center. Six people were killed and more than 1000 injured in that attack.

A Pakistani named Ramzi Yousef was eventually captured and convicted for that bombing, as were several Egyptians, including a blind Egyptian sheikh, Omar Abdel Rahman. According to the FBI, Yousef's 'specific choice of the World Trade Center as a target was due to his desire to topple one tower on to the other and cause a total of 250,000 civilian deaths. The heavy civilian loss of life would bring the attention of the American people to the plight of the Palestinians and cause America to realize that continued support of Israel would result in what was in effect a war.' The September 11 attacks were apparently carried out by al-Qaeda for similar reasons.

◄ **Afghan refugee families pass by armed Taliban militia near the Pakistan-Afghanistan border. Under Taliban law women were required to be covered from head to toe.**

▲ Police help injured workers flee from the World Trade Center on 26 February 1993, after a bomb exploded in the parking garage below ground.

▲ Water pours though the hole in the hull of the USS *Cole* after the ship was attacked by terrorists in Aden.

Earlier bin Laden attacks

Law enforcement officials believe bin Laden is responsible for two other major attacks on the USA.

On 7 August 1998 bombs exploded at US embassies in Kenya and in Tanzania. An embassy is the centre for a nation's diplomatic representatives to a foreign country. The attack destroyed the two embassy buildings and killed 224 people, including 12 Americans.

On 12 October 2000 the USS *Cole*, a navy destroyer, was refuelling in the harbour at Aden, a port city in Yemen, a small Arab country. Two men in a small rubber dinghy sailed alongside the *Cole* and detonated a bomb. The explosion blew a hole in the side of the *Cole*, killing 17 sailors, wounding 39 and disabling the destroyer.

Although bin Laden has never confirmed it, investigators believe al-Qaeda was responsible for both attacks.

Who is Osama bin Laden?

Osama bin Laden was born into a wealthy family in Saudi Arabia, probably in the late 1950s. His father, who died when Osama was about ten, was originally from Yemen and owned a large construction company.

Osama bin Laden could have stayed in Saudi Arabia and enjoyed the life of a rich man. As a teenager, he inherited an estimated US$25 million from the family fortune. In the 1980s, he went to Afghanistan to help the Afghan resistance – known as the mujahideen – against the Soviet Union, which had invaded the country in the 1980s. The mujahideen finally drove the Soviets out of Afghanistan in 1990.

▲ Osama bin Laden founded al-Qaeda.

Bin Laden returned to Saudi Arabia after the Afghanistan war. When Saudi Arabia allowed US troops to be stationed there during the US war against Iraq in 1991, bin Laden criticized the Saudi government. He then moved to the North African country of Sudan. There, he began to plan attacks against US targets, particularly in Somalia, where US troops had intervened in a civil war.

When Sudan's government asked bin Laden to leave in 1996, he returned to Afghanistan where the Taliban had taken control of the country. Grateful for his help to the mujahideen, the Taliban offered bin Laden shelter. In Afghanistan, bin Laden continued to organize and fund terrorist operations. He also allied al-Qaeda with numerous other terrorist groups around the globe. Investigators believe that terrorists linked to al-Qaeda operate in more than 60 countries.

Stories from ground zero

Sara Woster was working in her office on the 21st floor of the Woolworth Building, about one block from the World Trade Center, on the morning of September 11 2001. She was talking to colleagues when the aeroplane smashed into the north tower.

'We heard the impact,' said Woster. 'It sounded like a sonic boom, and although I don't remember if the building shook, you could physically feel the vibration of the impact in your body. It's like your stomach shook.'

Everyone in her office got up and went to the windows to see what was happening.

'We could see a huge, gaping hole with black smoke coming out of it,' Woster said. 'There was what looked like confetti falling all over, but in retrospect I'm sure we were fooled by the distance and it was really quite large pieces of metal. The fire trucks started going toward it below us within 30 seconds. We went up one floor above to watch CNN and that's when we were told that it was a plane and the smartest thing would be to stay inside and avoid being hit by debris.

'Then the second one hit and everybody started screaming and running because a fireball came right at the window. We realized this was no mistake and that we were being attacked. There was a very serious fear that as the next tallest building we could be the next target.

'We ran down the stairs and just took off walking north in small groups, criss-crossing the city to avoid landmarks and federal buildings. Our only news was when we would come upon small groups of people clustered around trucks listening to the radio. That's how we heard about the Pentagon.'

Woster was about 1 kilometre north of the site when the first tower collapsed. She thinks that seeing the crash from fairly close range may have helped her survive. Before the collapse, some people were actually walking towards the World Trade Center to see what was happening. Having been so close, Woster knew what had happened and that the smart thing to do was get away.

'We were close enough to see that entire floors were burning away and that the building would not be able to stay up,' Woster remembers. 'We were farther north for the second [collapse] and we knew what happened because everyone on the rooftops started pointing and crying and screaming and the ground shook.'

As Woster and her colleagues were trying to get away, a huge number of emergency vehicles were speeding toward the disaster. Police, firefighters and federal law enforcement agents were racing to the scene. She just wanted to get as far away as possible.

'Women and men were crying. Everyone was lining up at pay phones because our cellular [mobile] phones wouldn't work. There was no thought by anyone I talked to of "Who did this?" We were just trying to survive and worrying about the next possible target.'

Woster lives in Brooklyn, an area of New York City across the East River from Manhattan. She waited at a friend's apartment until 5:00 p.m. that afternoon, then walked over the Manhattan Bridge to her home. Subway and bus services had been shut down, so thousands of New Yorkers were walking home.

'There were people just covered in smoke and soot. It was completely silent except for sirens and the sounds of people walking. National Guard people were standing with machine guns every 2 feet

▲ **Police direct motorists away from Los Angeles International Airport following the terrorist attacks on the World Trade Center and the Pentagon. All US airports were to remain closed that day.**

with Red Cross workers handing out water every 3 feet. And when you stopped to look back you could only see the top of my building over the smoke,' Woster recalls.

Woster went back to work several days after the attacks, but things had changed. She had to pass through a number of security checkpoints each day to reach her office. 'It smells horrible,' she said more than a month after September 11, while the recovery work at the World Trade Center continued. 'Everyone wears dust masks. It's just very sad and physically exhausting.'

▲ New York firefighters stand at ground zero after the destruction of the World Trade Center.

A fireman's story

As the news spread throughout New York City of the devastation and destruction at the World Trade Center, the city's law enforcement and emergency agencies did what they are trained to do – they responded.

From all of New York City's five boroughs – Queens, Brooklyn, Staten Island, the Bronx and Manhattan itself – firefighters and their vehicles poured into lower Manhattan towards the site of the disaster.

The New York City Police Department responded in the same way, as did the officers of the Port Authority police and the city's many ambulance drivers and emergency medical workers.

So, while thousands of New Yorkers were rushing to get away from the burning, damaged twin towers, hundreds of police, firefighters and rescue workers were desperately trying to reach the scene of the catastrophe. Once there, the firefighters and police officers did what they do so often, although perhaps never on so large a scale – they rushed into the burning buildings, hoping to help as many people as possible to escape to the relative safety of the street. When the towers came down, 343 firefighters and 71 police officers were among those killed.

The New York City Fire Department lost all five of the city's elite rescue companies in their entirety. The entire personnel of 30 other companies were also missing.

As much as any of those who rushed to the disaster, Terence McShane embodied the qualities that enabled such a response. He had been both a firefighter and a policeman. As a member of Ladder Company 101 of the Fire Department, stationed in Red Hook, Brooklyn, Terence was among the first firefighters to arrive at the scene. His truck was emerging from the mouth of the Brooklyn-Battery Tunnel when the members of his company saw the second aeroplane smash into the south tower.

The details of what happened then are mostly unknown, except that the members of Company 101 rushed into the south tower and none of them came out alive. Though Terence McShane was 37 years old, he had only been with the New York Fire Department for a few years. Before that, he had spent 12 years as a New York City policeman, reaching the rank of sergeant. He switched to the Fire Department because the change would allow him to spend more time with his wife and three young sons.

The recovery effort

Before September 11 2001, 'ground zero' was a term used to mean 'the place directly above, below, or at which a nuclear explosion occurs.' Ground zero has only been in the language for a little more than 50 years. It was first used in 1945, the year in which atomic weapons were used in war for the only time in the world's history. In August of that year, the US airforce dropped atomic bombs on the Japanese cities of Hiroshima and Nagasaki to bring about an end to World War II. The destruction and loss of life was enormous, and the areas closest to the explosions were completely destroyed. These areas became known as 'ground zero'.

After September 11, ground zero took on a new meaning in the USA. It was used to refer to the place where the twin towers of the World Trade Center once stood. Left above ground was a horrifying tangle of metal, concrete, glass, paper, plastic, dust and debris in huge heaps of rubble. Some of the worst damage was below ground level in the form of collapsed subway tunnels and crushed automobiles from the WTC's underground parking garages. Huge pieces of concrete and iron weighing as much as 30 tons had been driven down by the force of the collapse, yet some offices and stores below ground level remained almost intact. Fires burned non-stop and clouds of smoke and steam drifted amid the wreckage. Within all this destruction were the remains of nearly 3000 people trapped by the disaster.

Three months after the attack thousands of recovery workers, many of them volunteers, continued to work in shifts that lasted throughout the night and day. They worked seven days a week to clear away the rubble and discover the missing. In doing so, they ran the risk of becoming additional casualties of the tragedy.

Fires continued to burn below ground. With each shift, the recovery workers breathed in what was described as a 'deadly soup of dust, gases, burning chemicals and potentially toxic compounds,' including asbestos and **PCB**. Among other things, ground zero was now the site of a major oil spill. More than 130,000 gallons of oil were released when two electrical power stations were destroyed in the collapse. Workers at the site were risking serious long-term damage to their health by working in such a hostile environment.

▲ **A US flag flies at half-mast over ground zero.**

Even so, few of them intended to give up. Three months later much of the damage above ground had been cleared. Some 600,000 tons of steel and debris had been moved away. But of the nearly 3000 people left missing in the disaster, only a handful had been rescued alive in the first few days after the attack. The rest were presumed dead; by late December, the remains of fewer than 600 of them had been recovered. In a short time on that fateful Tuesday morning, a small area of lower Manhattan had simultaneously become ruins, a crime scene, the site of a major environmental disaster and a graveyard.

Looking ahead: war on terrorism

Very soon after terrorists struck the World Trade Center and the Pentagon on September 11 2001, US leaders called the attacks an act of war. Four days after the airliners were **hijacked**, President George W. Bush said the US military was prepared for a long struggle to fight **terrorism**.

'We're at war,' the president told the American people on 15 September. 'There's been an act of war declared upon America by terrorists, and we will respond accordingly.' Bush told the American people that this war would not be like past conflicts. There would be no front lines. 'Victory,' Bush said, 'will not take place in a single battle, but in a series of decisive actions against terrorist organizations and those who harbour and support them.'

New York firefighters placed a US flag on what was left of the collapsed towers of the World Trade Center.

▲ **Afghan refugee women and children wait in line for shelter near the Jalozai camp in the North-West Frontier province of Pakistan. More than 30 per cent of Afghanistan's people have been made refugees by war and famine in the last 20 years.**

From the very beginning, the US government maintained the chief suspect was Osama bin Laden, who was still living in Afghanistan. Bush demanded that the government of Afghanistan, the Taliban, turn over bin Laden. The Taliban refused.

On 7 October 2001, the USA and the UK launched powerful missiles and dropped bombs on targets in Afghanistan. Jets from aircraft carriers and long-range bombers dropped laser-guided bombs. Cruise missiles were launched from submarines. Soon after the bombing, US 'special forces' troops moved into Afghanistan. These special forces troops found targets for the bombers and helped the Northern Alliance, an Afghan military group opposed to the Taliban. By the end of November, the Taliban had been driven from power, although bin Laden was still at large, said to be hiding deep in remote caves in eastern Afghanistan.

President Bush tried to get as many countries as possible to support the US action. Many did, including some Islamic countries, such as Pakistan, which allowed the USA to use bases in their country. Other countries declined to help. Bush said the attacks on Afghanistan were not directed against Muslims but against terrorists. 'We are the friends of almost a billion [people] worldwide who practise the Islamic faith,' the president said. Instead, he said the attacks on Afghanistan should be understood as the first strikes in a war against terrorism.

▲ **Candles flicker at a memorial for victims of the World Trade Center attack in Brooklyn, across the East River from Manhattan.**

Afghanistan and war

Afghanistan has been the scene of almost unending warfare since 1980. For more than ten years Afghan resistance fighters, aided by Muslims, fought the Soviet occupation of their country. These fighters were known as mujahideen. Once the Soviets were driven out, various mujahideen groups fought each other for control of the country's government – with the Taliban eventually winning. Grateful for his help against the Soviets, the Taliban provided a haven for bin Laden and al-Qaeda. At first most of the people of Afghanistan welcomed the Taliban because they ended the civil war. But then the leaders enforced new rules upon society based on an extremely strict interpretation of the Koran.

Under Taliban rule, women had to keep their head and face covered at all times. Women were not allowed to hold jobs or go to school. Many people left the country to get away from the restrictions on their life. People who violated the rules were arrested and sometimes killed.

The harshness of the Taliban rule meant that many Afghans were not sad to see the Taliban defeated by the USA and its Afghan allies. This did not mean, however, that the Afghans were united about who should take the Taliban's place.

Afghanistan is home to many different ethnic groups, or peoples. With the Taliban gone, many Afghans feared that the end of the US war against al-Qaeda, whenever that took place, would be followed by another civil war in Afghanistan, as different ethnic groups stuggled for power.

◀ **Children in Afghanistan pause as they sift through war ruins in Kabul, the capital city of Afghanistan.**

Long-term impact of the September attacks

There is no doubt that the attacks on the World Trade Center changed life in the USA. People worried about more terrorist attacks and the future of their country. Soldiers patrolled airports and landmarks across the country.

Law enforcement officials were given new powers – for example, to **wiretap** telephone conversations. Many Arab immigrants were held for questioning without being charged for a crime. President Bush signed an **executive order** allowing suspected terrorists captured by the USA to be tried in secret military **tribunals**, where the usual rules of evidence would not apply.

By the end of 2001, US bombing raids and ground operations had helped the Taliban's opponents drive it from power. The search for bin Laden, who had been believed to be hiding in caves in eastern Afghanistan, carried on. Americans were wondering if the war on terror was soon to involve the US military in battle against other Arab nations such as Iraq. The World Trade Center and Pentagon attacks, which were the most destructive acts committed on the US mainland by a foreign enemy since the War of 1812, had made the USA a very different place.

'Americans have known surprise attacks, but never before on thousands of civilians,' President Bush said in his speech to **Congress** following the attacks. 'All of this was brought upon us in a single day, and night fell on a different world.'

Texas National Guard troops stand at a security post inside a terminal at the Dallas-Fort Worth International Airport in Grapevine, Texas, on 6 October 2001. As part of increased security measures, National Guard soldiers were deployed to patrol US airports. ►

Countries that lost citizens in the WTC attacks

Antigua & Barbuda
Argentina
Australia
Austria
Bahamas
Bangladesh
Barbados
Belgium
Belarus
Belize
Bolivia
Brazil
Cambodia
Canada
Chile
China
Colombia
Costa Rica
Czech Republic
Dominica
Dominican Republic
Ecuador
Egypt
El Salvador
France
Germany
Ghana
Greece
Guatemala
Guyana
Haiti
Honduras
Hong Kong
India

Indonesia
Iran
Ireland
Israel
Italy
Jamaica
Japan
Jordan
Kenya
Lebanon
Luxembourg
Malaysia
Mexico
Morocco
The Netherlands
New Zealand
Nicaragua
Norway
Pakistan
Panama
Paraguay
Peru
Philippines
Poland
Portugal
Romania

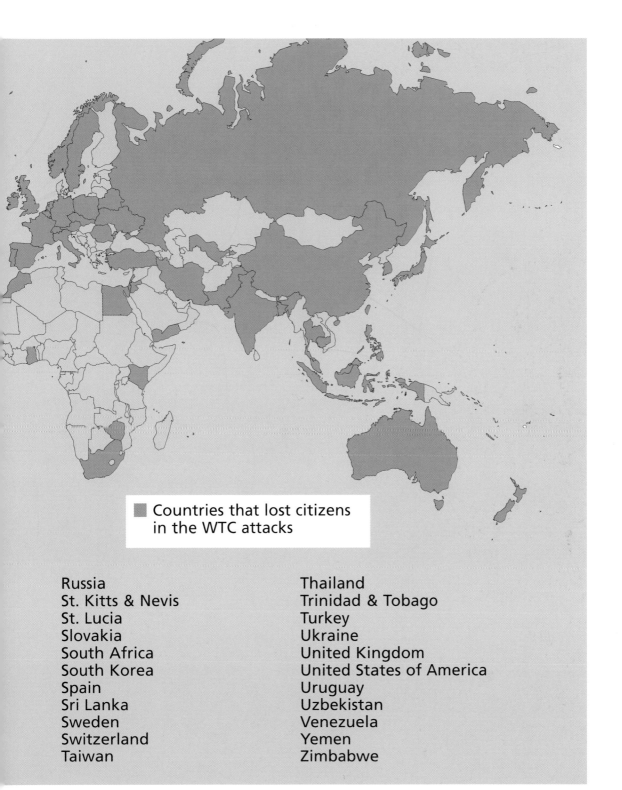

Countries that lost citizens in the WTC attacks

Russia	Thailand
St. Kitts & Nevis	Trinidad & Tobago
St. Lucia	Turkey
Slovakia	Ukraine
South Africa	United Kingdom
South Korea	United States of America
Spain	Uruguay
Sri Lanka	Uzbekistan
Sweden	Venezuela
Switzerland	Yemen
Taiwan	Zimbabwe

Glossary

Congress official law-making body of the USA

executive order directive issued by a US president that is not voted on by the US Congress

extremism/extremists going to great, unusual or excessive lengths to achieve a goal; people who do this

fundamentalist extremely strict or literal interpretation of a religion's sacred books and teachings

hijack to take illegal control of a plane or other vehicle in order to force it to go somewhere

martyr someone who is killed or made to suffer because of his or her beliefs

PCB polychlorinated biphenyl – toxic compound formed as waste in some industrial processes

prophet person who speaks or claims to speak for God; a person who predicts what will happen in the future

refugee person forced to leave his or her home due to war, persecution, or a natural disaster

terrorism the use of acts that cause fear and terror in an attempt to achieve political and/or religious goals

tribunal court of law

wiretap to secretly connect into a communications circuit to listen in on another's conversations

Resources

http://news.bbc.co.uk

Visit this website to keep up-to-date with the latest news from around the world.

www.timeforkids.com

Type 'world trade center' into the quick search field, to find up-to-date articles from the USA, as a nation remembers September 11 2001.

www.yahooligans.com

Type any key words – from 'World Trade Center' to '9.11.01' – and choose from a list of top sites that provide a history of terrorism, up-to-date information for students and forums to express feelings about the tragedy.

www.pbs.org/empires/islam

An overview of Islam that is brief and easy to understand. Learn about Islam's history and traditions and about the religion today.

Disclaimer

All the Internet addresses (URLs) given in this book were valid at the time of going to press. However, due to the dynamic nature of the Internet, some addresses may have changed, or sites may have ceased to exist since publication. While the author and publishers regret any inconvenience this may cause, no responsibility for any such changes can be accepted by either the author or the publishers.

Further reading

Troubled World: Arab-Israeli Conflict, Ivan Minnis (Heinemann Library, May 2001)

Witness to History: 11 September 2001, Brendan January (Heinemann Library, Autumn 2003)

Index

Afghanistan, 6, 22, 28, 38, 39, 41, 42
al-Qaeda, 21, 22, 24, 25, 27, 28, 41
al-Wahhab, Muhammad ibn, 25

bin Laden, Osama, 6, 21, 22, 27, 28,
    38, 39, 41, 42
Burnett, Thomas E., 15
Bush, George W., 6, 7, 9, 10, 36, 38,
    39, 42

Egypt, 22, 25

India, 23
Indonesia, 20
Iraq, 28, 42
Islam, 20–25, 39
Israel, 22–25

Judaism, 20

Kenya, 27
Koran, 20, 21, 24, 41

Middle East, 22, 23
mujahideen, 28, 41
Muslim, 20–24, 29, 39

Northern Alliance, 38

Pakistan, 23, 25, 39
Palestinian, 23, 25
Petit, Phillippe, 18

Qutb, Sayyid, 22

Saudi Arabia, 6, 22, 27, 28
Somalia, 28
Soviet Union, 22, 28
Sudan, 28

Taliban, 22, 28, 38, 39, 41, 42
Tanzania, 27

UK, 38
USS Cole, 27

Willig, George, 18
Woster, Sara, 29–31

Yamasaki, Minoru, 17, 18, 19
Yemen, 27, 28
Yousef, Ramzi, 25